NEW

HORIZONS

NEW

HORIZONS

Selected poems from 50 years

DEVIN ALARIC MIKLES

MOON AND STAR PRESS

SEDONA, ARIZONA

New Horizons
Selected Poems from 50 years

For permission to reprint certain poems,
I would like to thank the editors of
The Collared Peccary

Front and back cover photo: Charles Ruscher
www.absoluteinspiration.com

Design by Artline Graphics, Sedona AZ, USA.
www.artline-graphics.com

ISBN 9781698363967

BISAC:
Literary Collections / American / General
Nonfiction / Poetry / American / General

For the Divine Mother

and the Divine Father ......

in deepest gratitude,

and for my Mother, who loved me well,

and my Father

who shared his love of nature, books,

writing and poetry.

Treasure

My gold is beggars' gold
That's found beside the road.
It's daisies, buttercups and such;
Jade streams and bubble pearls,
Ruby buds and turquoise skies,
And clouds of raveled fleece
That float in hazel sunset fires
Like tired, wind-tossed butterflies.

A burnished disk of marigold,
Apple trees hung with blood,
A tune played by ivory-fingered winds
On strings
Of weeping willow or laughing aspen,
Is the rainbow pot
I seek beyond the horizon.

> Truman Fredrick Mikles
> Crescent City, California
> Circa 1947

TABLE OF

CONTENTS

I

The Poet's Body

The Poet

He pens of many a line,
Charts the patterns of the stars,
And shows them all to rhyme.
Flows hues of skies and chimes of bells
To form a verse sublime.
Traces shadows of lovers
Illumined by the rising moon.
Smells sweet nectars
Sitting 'neath the orchard trees at noon.
Binds sheaves of joy and laughter
From the ever-filling room.

But when the hand of the penner
Grows to sleep from write,
And evening creeps a misty light,
And snuggles up to night,
He closes tangible and visible tightly from his sight,
Seeks to serve the Muses well,
And open wisdom's gate.

Poetry Lesson #2

Just the simple ramblings of the mind
With no contrived boundaries to be used.
Plain ordinary imagination on no line.
Loose forth all fantasy and things mused.
Array the finest treasure you can find;
Bother not to order, pick, or choose.
Trust bare facts as they reveal themselves in time
Matters not they come in fours or threes or twos.
Write, save all, and save them for a rhyme.
Strive not to set together, set them loose.
Poetry is for people of all kind,
Forged by persons strong, mild, and obtuse.
Therefore, by no established poets be beguiled.
A sonnet can be written by a child.

Epitaph

Only the poet's body in death's grip lies
To be celebrated or not in bright verses
The true Spirit of Healing joyous flies
Loving infinite through the Universes!

II

Songs of Nature

GORDIAN MAZE

Water threaded lime walls;
Multifarious sandstone passages
Reverberate, answer hiker's quandary:
Follow anywhere the fine filigree design;
It is always the canyon.

LYNX RUFUS

Living close to the city
Though seldom seen.
Occasionally at the dump
His prowling green eyes
Stir excitement in a rag-picker.
Padded with claws, he paws softly;
Cautiously avoiding corrupted humanity.
Tufted pinnae twitch in anticipation of prey;
He must kill.
It is his way;
Even if not for food.
The kill gives life.
His muscular tawny frame shines
As he flashes in the pines.
Playful as he appears,
Romping with Rufus requires
Prudence and a sense of respect.

ORGAN RIDDLE

Pulse.
Control pulsates.
Rhythm chambers undulate.
Outside, glistening light waves.
Inside, dark halls of valvule channels
Feed and draw.
Vital fluxion drives, grows,
And renews.
Symbol of mystic peace.
Cyclic dancer:
Self-feeding seat of life.

WASUSU LANDSCAPE

Plush jungle wades tree-deep
To caverned foothills, where
Millennia-old vampire bat guano
Buries petroglyphs of the Sun God,
Dancing tapir and anteater. Above,
The Mato Grosso plateau whistles
Sand whirldevils and the high passes
Of Abrigo del Sol cast the shadow
Of my grandfather's Dreaming on all this.

Schrödinger's Dream: Natures Answer

Through a sea of bioplasmic ethers
Emerges a figure in white radiance;
Distinctly living, scintillating,
Aperiodic crystal. Long twisted strands;
A succession of tiny isomeric units.
Living light revealing itself as
The life and immortal twinkle
From which the entire of humankind
And most living organisms come.
The universal code, personalization,
Incarnation, germinally complete,
Map and key to the field of manifestation,
The everlasting embryo and completer,
Preserver of purity and *perfection*.

According to James D. Watson's memoir, *DNA, The Secret of Life*, Schrödinger's 1944 book What is Life? gave Watson the inspiration to research the gene, which led to the discovery of the DNA double helix structure.

Erwin Schrödinger. His great discovery, *Schrödinger's wave equation,* was made during the first half of 1926. It came as a result of his dissatisfaction with the quantum condition in Bohr's orbit theory and his belief that atomic spectra should really be determined by an eigenvalue problem. For this work he shared with Dirac the Nobel Prize for 1933.

From *Nobel Lectures*, Physics 1922-1941.

WHAT QUADRAVITATIS SEES

High in the country above,
Clouds roll up the valley
Surging slow motion
As a foamy foggy sea
Upon the isles of evergreen shores;
With sprays of golden showered
Upon the valley floors.

It is the dragon of winter
Blowing up the hills.
That downy breath
Straightens the spines
Of the rock dwellers.

Evening shows a silent sea
That covers the land,
Hides the men,
Rests the mind,
Reflects the rising moon.

CHEETAH
(aka Cat Food)

SEE SPOTS.
SEE SPOTS RUN.
BLURR...
GAZELLE,
GAZELLE NO MORE.

SAVANNAH HEAT
DRIES THE GORE
THAT SOAKS THE SOIL,
THAT BUGS WILL ROLL UP SEEDS IN,
RAINS WILL SPROUT UP TREES, AND
NEW BABES WILL EAT THE LEAVES FROM;

SO SPOTS CAN RUN
GAZELLES THROUGH FIELDS
FULL OF YELLOW FLOWERS.

Butterfly

From the primordial core of my being,
An urgent passion and longing
Gels and extrudes.
Reaching out and up, in and down and through.
Screaming, crying forth the sound of the unborn.

Though I have been locked within
The coffin of my ignorance and inability
To Metamorphosize,
I have refused this silent death,
Sensing my Chrysalis forming in the Spirit realm,
It is calling out for me to enter,
Become a new embodiment.

Did you see the morning?

Smell of pine wood burning
Lazily creaking crickets
Churn the darkness at 4:11
Incense and lemon grass smoking

In the haze at the crack of dawn
Thuja trees sway, "me too!"
And all the little birds pipe in
To let the lovers know

The Mother hears their peace
Feels their love
Growing and enfolding all things
Living, living, living

Swing out with the song
Of the devoted heart
Longing for the voice
Of the sacred silence

Birthing the palette
Of the blushing day flower
The peace of connection
Is mind stopping...

Little Bear, Laughing Raven

I'd look up for Orion
Sit in caves and look for light
Sleep in fields all through the summer
Count the stars all though the night

Little bear climbing in the tree
Raven circles laughing at me
Little bear climbing in the tree
Raven circles laughing at me

Teaching me that the Earth
Is the living body of the Spirit
Along with all the Universe
Sprang from the grace of just one nod

Little bear are you calling to me
Raven are you circling to see
Little bear are you calling to me
Raven are you circling to see

Through the Peace of Understanding
Bring true union through the strife
Loving is the passion that
Binds us to this life

When it seems that the path
Turns to the wrong
The journey is not through
Celebrate the moment
For there is more for us to do

Oh, peace come to us now
As the winding strains the vow
Speak to me, oh speak to me

Sitting in the garden
In the space that we created
Searching for the answer
Of this love we have been fated

Little bear are you listening to me
Raven is there wisdom in the circle you see
Little bear are you listening to me
Raven is there wisdom in the circle you see

I'm calling for the angel
To come into this place
Take the worry from your brow
Put a smile upon your face

Little bear laughing in the tree
Raven circles smiling at me
Little bear laughing in the tree
Raven circles smiling at me

The Copperheads

The field lay quiet in the foggy morning.
Parched frozen remnants of broken hay stems
Crunching under my feet.
Deep in the ground beneath
The sleeping slithers sighed, and
My boy face smiled from safety.

Tramping in the spring mud
To a dark deep hole near the utility pole
Where they lay in a tangled mass writhing
Slick in a nest of shed slack skins;
Maybe 20 casting the gall of fear
And careful, trepid wonder; considering
The design of their effective removal
From wandering little feet in the meadow.

Memories of a buzzing summer day
High in the Blue Ridge;
Stepping lightly on the edge of the granite cliff,
The command to run came suddenly,
And looking back I saw him slink swiftly
Across the burnished trail,
My footprint interrupted by the course of his passing,
My heart in my stomach.

Dead in the road, mingling
With the red and orange leaves,
Natural in repose, now harmless and beautiful,
I pause to consider also
How fragile are the poisonous ones;
How time takes in passage
Even the semblant most evil of us.

The Doldrums

It seemed a merry time was had
And seemed t'would be forever
Waves of glowing, blissful light
And thoughts were oh so clever.

In winter's gloom there was no room
Or reason to be down
The grace of spring trades filled the sails
And counseled to the crown

Now safely past the horsey latitudes
The mind did start to fix on
Glory days and stellar nights
In waves so sure to press on

So now it comes as such surprise
When winds do cease to blow
For every time it happens
We're chagrined to find it so

A state of inactivity said
The mind we find is bored
And all the drivel we have stored
Has risen from the seabed
So listless now we rocked and swayed
In listless reverie we
Mock with yowls and moans replayed
A dreary caw and plea

Alas for now there's no relief
From depression and from humdrums
So welcome fellow sailor
To your vacation in the doldrums!

Snake Eyes

Shakti comes to visit
And the primordial sight
Fosters volumes of fear.

What is it in that
Primes the sympathetic
Response to attention?

Ages old, locked
In the racial, cellular
Genetic, karmic vehicle,

Terror comes of
Its own volition,
Unbalancing the thoughtful.

When we see thousands
Maimed and murdered
On the screen nightly,

And we are dulled
To a zombie glare
Poached in the miasma,

This is the shame;
Not the casual natural
Response to the slither brother!

July 4

Golden colored silence, the afternoon
Is made of crystalline sparkles.

Only a bell and a bird break the stillness...
It seems that the two talk with the setting sun.

A roving purity sways the cool trees,
Releasing the visions of ten thousand elementals
To penetrate throughout the wood.

And beyond all that,
A transparent river dreams
That trampling over pearls,
It breaks loose
And flows into infinity.

III

Friendship

We Sat In The Park

We sat in the park,
The children and I;
Watching the leaves fall
Watching the people pass,
Listening to the rhythmic play of the sprinklers,
And refreshed by the mist of spray;
That golden sunlit day,
Mindless, timeless, skyless day;
Moonlit by the waning moon
And the waiting passes,
And the children feel an old man's life
And turn to pass on.

A walk in the snow

A walk in the snow
To a place of expressible peace,
Sense-able, and reachable.
Beauty that is real - beyond our time,
Touchable enough to habituate its' desire.
And ...a guide showing the way through contrast.

The element of discrimination; while
At the same time acting like acid
Falling upon an unstable substance;
Slowly, almost painfully running the colors of
The psychic painting together;
Sending all to oblivion and concurrently producing
A wealth of new experience, knowledge, sensation and desire.

The dichotomy of this affliction is the secret we share;
Like the silent falling of snow upon the city,
And the high passes of distant mountains.

FOREVER MAGIC

I'll oft remember friends well met,
Who worked and toiled without restraint.
Their love and laughter filled me through,
Like the song of the nightingale as it echoes across my garden.

A starfilled night, that evening so named "magic time."
It came and seven times there after brought my spirits higher.
Love's labours won were counted, love's labours lost discharged.
A new life runs through my soul, my freedom runs to meet it.
Like a newborn wind upon the loose.

These simple lines cannot explain,
Nor tell of love's deep change.
But all the myriad affections felt by all
Shall remain within our common heart;
There lies the magic book of truth
Where all are free to gaze.

Friendvessel

 Oh, to be tethered
On some sailing ship
Off island paradise
Upon a blue-green turtle sea
That's sparkling and placid.
Instead I sit here
Morrassed suburban prisoner
In belching noise and fumes
From megalith machines
That smelt the rain to acid.

Your friendship of plain sweetness
That some consider lightly,
Trite and mundane;
Without which wild-eyed,
My wits had parted and
I should have been insane,
Is the long-lost vessel
Of my soul;
It's harbor I now claim.

Invocation

Flight of the healing Spirit
In evershining release
To the profound journey
For the sweet medicine
Human being blessing
Soul reflection dance,
Song of transformation
In the clear oracle of self,
On a love quest,
Into the tender night,
Mysterious Earth womb of light
Paradox of peace envelop your life.

In The House Of My Belonging

And by that road we came home,
Arm in arm,
Heart to heart;
Undisturbed by the past
And din of the time that was.
And before us lay the way
With a lightness of being
Numinous to the core,
Wet with tears and sparkling!

I came from there to here.
From there where I was them and saw
Through the eyes that missing me,
I came to know but could not see.
In the mirror of their eyes, I saw my light
And here I am to be
For now, and here to be
In the house of my belonging.

In This Circle I Belong

In this circle I belong.
There is only this:
That we came here to love
And to be loved
In the place of our own choosing,
Well met and together
By the light of the Soul.

Careening nations
Bent on the edge of catastrophe
Could not dull the purpose
of our Peace
For incorruptible are we
That stand bound
By the glistening of the cosmos.

Starward and beyond,
As the ring passes,
I will never forget to remember
All of you,
And the greatness
That you brought
To this place.

About A Life...A Work In Progress

Winter solstice midnight in the pine forest
He came the morning after
He was made
Presenting to the morning meditation
Welcomed with surprise
Unsure of our feelings
He had waited years
For that unprotected moment
An opening to life.

Yet when he was formed
At the Autumnal equinox
And all was in readiness
He was not as sure
Drawn from the womb
With a knife
And a freshness that is indescribable
Known only to the initiated
Awake and silent he came into this world.

As I laid him in the arms
Of his most beloved
Their eyes locked in
A long and deep knowing
Caught me unprepared

And for a while he was content
To be here in this place.

In the bosom of the family
At three he told us
He called out "I want to go home.
I want to go home."
Where is that?
Where is that?
He could not say
He could not say
Not of this world.

I am a Jupiterian
He told us later
I go there at night
When everyone is sleeping.
But it is OK here sometimes
Sometimes he can not bear the painful parts
"Don't look, don't touch!"
"I hurt my thumb-toe"
Now we walk together in the pine forest
Liking the silence
And the sound of the flute
Smell of the Earth
Feeling of the ground against our moccasins
Call of the raven
The spaces between knowing and not
What comes next?

A Transition

(for two voices – male boldly in a regular cadence
and female *[quietly, brightly and slowly]*)

The Earth Dance is Over
[drumming is heard in the distance]
The Dancer will Rest
He takes off His Earth Shoes
[dust falls in yellow petal clouds]
Now He Breathes with an Invisible Breath
[hair stands up your neck]
Walks with Invisible Tracks
[foot prints appear momentarily on your soul]
Speaks in a Voice I can only Hear In My Heart
[Spirit Heart beating in the Rhythms of the Universe]
He speaks in a Sacred Voice
[Mitakuye Oyasin Wakan Tanka Nici Un]
Walks the Sacred Walk
[A path to your heart opens]
Breathes the Peaceful Sigh in My Mind
[a porpoise song echoes across the still waters]
In My Minds Eye He is Dancing in the Mist
[Mana is the Life Force that destroys all obstacles]
Of the Great Spirit
[Sacred Bells Ring Out Rhyming with the Dawn]
Dancing the Sacred Dance
[Eternity is Now!]

IV

Live Life Sketches

WEATHERMAN

Within the distant thundering of reefs,
Harbor silence covers the village.
Old Rdjka knows, as he carries the last
Wet net up to the hut, the rising red moon
Brings heavy rain, and early morning fog harbor.
The nets will remain dry tomorrow.
Rdjka will smoke his pipe on the porch.

Geisha

Once with four attendants to wash her body with
Oils and perfumes; comb and braid her hair, trim,
Powder and pamper her while she mused about the
Special men that would come to her in the evening
To be flattered and pleased and dazzled by her
Incredibly, perfect poise, grace, intelligence
And manners, now her wrinkled and callused hands
Pound rice daily for her old mistress in the kitchen.

Eldila

At times of the solitary transition from love,
We resemble the Eldila; neither angel nor demon,
But in the mirror, a phantom, revealing the surface
Of a body which exists after a manner beyond
Our conception; flamelike but dull. We see a
Frame lacking the multidimensional geometry of a
Living person that we know must exist somewhere
In the celestial reference. Now at these moments,
We could well slip into the world of Faerie easily,
Delighting in the mischievousness for wont of a real
Heart.

CHIEF JOSEPH

Monadic, nomadic, tenuous,
Wizened old man
Gives up his body
Leaving bondage,
A decaying culture
To his descendants.
He does not understand.
Neither do they.

A MASTER

Ryokan lived the simplest life
At the foot of the hill
In a small hut.

A thief comes to visit
And finds nothing;
Ryokan returns.

He had come a long way
To return empty handed,
So Ryokan gave him his
Only clothes.

Later when he sat naked
By the hut watching the sky
He wished that he could have given
The poor fellow the beautiful moon.

Holy Man: He Who Knows Love

Laughing warrior,
[And he would be the first to say]
Always striving to live the simplest life,
Tricking the coyote.

Naked in the river of life,
[Touching the Divine]
Drinking all that he can of experience,
But not for satiety sake

Dancing crazy wisdom,
[Abandoning all he has]
Feisty kangaroo jig,
A gurgling giggle of graciousness.

Evermore giving thanks,
[Fundamentally piercing devachan]
Master of the sacred gratuity,
Living proof of deep touching.

It was when I looked into the eyes
[Stop! The Beauty!]
Of his beloveds that I knew
The truth of his becoming.

This is a heart that knows love.
[A cosmic fool rushes]
He showed it to me
In the willows, the sand like stars.

I saw it in everything he touched,
[Shivers of surrender]
Passion flowing as water,
Abundant, filling everything it passes.

And no one calls him sage to his face.
[He would just laugh!]
A peace that has no name.

If you walk even a small space
[May fortune smile on you]
In his flamboyant footsteps
You will know real compassion.

The Hospice Candidate

His life was
Bartered between specialists
Fragmented into organ systems
Displayed in graphic test reports
Explored in the disease specific database
Discussed in hushed tones and esoterica
Recorded in tomes and
Stored on a dusty shelf

Still he came
Smiling into the light of his day
Even with a problem list as long as your arm
He presented with grace and
Was grateful for his breath
Each stride on the earth precious
The vital essence of all things
Imprinted in his consciousness

At the allotted
Time he made his way
Offering solace to those that would stay
Pouring peace and a shining countenance
On the gathered, on their worried way
And in the last gasp he exclaimed
"Daddy, come and get me now! I'm not kiddin'!"

SPEAK OF IT THEN

Family bonds extrude, extend the phase
Where the Moon faces the Sun.
Here in the House of Pain, I wait,
For Death to release the sparkle
Of a Mother's life.

Unwittingly we slide across a hidden guide;
Making decisions that only the initiated can avoid
In traversing the bland landscape that shifts
Without warning above the abyss.

These are Life's lessons and we
Are the blind architects of our own Plan
Locked in an expanding anthropic universe;
Is there meaning or is there dust?

Who thinks he knows may or may not.
The Heart may know but cannot speak.
Of what value Hope or Faith?
Rescue is not clear, but time and space
have no limits...

V

Earth Tones

"The important thing is this: to be able at a moment's notice
to sacrifice what we are for what we could become."

Charles du Bos

New Horizons

When the peak of experience provides us with opportunity,
The peace of the heart is required.
To have that available to us in the moment,
Is the key to right decision.
The leap of faith remands us to our destiny,
For the greater and not the lesser,
And there is no turning back.

In the cave of generation,
It is difficult to see the blueprint of the future.
One must know that they are a Creator,
And that the will of the Universe stands with them.
To be a visionary is no small task,
For one must swallow the small bile of fear,
And strike forth from the depth of Soul with surety.

"Boys throw stones at frogs in sport,
but the frogs do not die in sport.
They die in earnest."

From Plutarch, Water and Land Animals, Greek Biographer, First Century CE

Venus in Tights

History do you hold your course?
Protracted, agonizing suffering...
Those who ring the bells of warning
Long cold and dead in the grave
Before heed was taken.
Status quo world of human consciousness.
Those who see the way
Never seen as the way shower
Until the knell is past the finish.
The path of pain and death that brings awakening persists.
For those who do not see, most difficult the darkness.
Find the courage to proceed,
Honor the truth of social and human injustice.
This short life where
We are not bound to serve;
Our free will to choose;
How well will we do this:
Sitting in a cave or cabin and meditate/pray/radiate;
Down into the din of the marketplace
Giving succor to the masses;
Stand for them when they lack the fortitude...

No shame or blame and no spiritual fame for either path.
Truly nothing here that matters in the greater cosmic scheme.
No cleverness, invention or intervention
Can change the final outcome,
But in our compassion as self-accepted agents of Will,
We made the choice to serve in our way
This Star of Suffering.
Look back and see that it is good,
Powerless in the wake of the terrible
Wretched payout that reeks and reels
From the hate of brother upon brother.
Small as we feel and as we truly are,
Faithful to the cause of Joy,
Even if we burn in the fire of human tragedy.
As the final curtain falls,
Hear the thunder of angels, and travel on.
Cosmos is eternal.

Rocking with the Wind

Beneath the crust of you
Men toiled to bring up the black rock
That fired the cold blue metal
That brought me here today
To watch the wind waving the trees in our Sun
Setting with the rising of the harvest Moon
And the brilliance of the evening planets

Seeing this I felt
Your strength course through all of it
All of us

Parts of us like you
Are in the dark soiled and toiling
Others in the light
All here together to make this Human body
That in its expressions reaches for the Ultimate

Each is needed to do this
There are no seconds or thirds
Only singular unique expressions of you

As I watch the innocents at play
Those who slog in the muck
Or sit in grassy meadows
Others who climb to the spires of the cities
Labor in the depths of the factories
It is your breath that breathes there

And we are all woven together
In a seamless fabric of beingness

Connected

We each must choose to accept that
which we are guided to do in our heart of hearts.

I feel a part of this dear planet.
I am of it.
I groan with it;
breathe with it the living air and aether.
I sway in its embrace.
Yes, I speak to the trees and talk to the rocks.
The grass and the moss are my lovers;
all creatures my sisters and brothers.
There is no part of its joy or misery that I do not feel.
But, I hide from myself and from you, that painful reality.
To face it straight on would mean annihilation to this small and
insignificant frame;
this pitiful and small mind.

That this sweet Mother of our physical bodies
would reveal anything to us of substance,
or continue to forbear in our presence here
after the abuse that we have piled upon her,
and continue to lay on,
is nothing short of a total mystery.
Yet, She bears all and carries all
in tolerance and with prudence.

There is a definitive process of communication
to those who have "ears to hear and eyes to see";
a message of acceptance.
Acceptance of a plea;
a cry from the heart of Man
to "let there be relief."

Let there be relief!
Relief of the ancient evil that binds us
to irrational thinking
that we are here alone
separate from other beings.

No one and no thing
can stop the light now.
They will still try,
but as of today
there is no way back into the darkness
for those whose eyes are open.

The lines are drawn!
The road is set!
We remember.
We release.
We relinquish.

We reset.
We forgive.
We heal.
We love.

The Sacredness of Porpoises

I looked into your face
But there was anger
Despair, distrust, dismay.

I saw the pain and the fear there,
And it smelled like rotting food.

I thought I didn't know you
And you frightened me,
But I continued to look
Because I knew you must be there.

Behind the terrible, terrified torture
Of your countenance,
You must be there.

There I waited and
Stilled my heart.
Red lingering sunsets
Rows of purple coneflowers
Spilling onto the horizon.

In the calm of the morning
Through the busy day
I finally felt you.

Tall pines wafted
By the breezes of summer.

Like an angel you touched my soul
Blessed me with
Your forgiveness
Limitless mounds of grain
Reaching the mouths of the starving.

I was at peace.
With the courage of a lion
But the sedate repose
Of the Koala.

Tenderness and patience
Was your lesson plan.
Given the sacredness
Of porpoises.

In The Darkness Of The New Moon

Peace!
In the darkness of the new moon,
The jeweled peaks are silent and hidden
In the mystery of the night.
Though Xanadu may still exist
In the mind of fantasy,
There can be no mistake
That the beauty my heart desires
Remains far more fragile a creation.

Flights of fancy cannot escape
The reality of day where all of the blemishes
Of the world in turmoil find their
Place upon the stage
Of this haunted planet
And a vast fatigue descends
Visiting exhaustion on this visage.

Is there a new world to be born
Of the haste and waste that pours
From the gutters of this one?
Or will humanity be deadly silenced by
The careening of misdirected
Parallel lines of manifesting desire?
Or indeed is there a meaning for any of it
Other than acquisition of new awareness?

In the cancellation of minds and forms
Can there be a salvage of any one thing of value
To the creating force that overlies
The incarnating creation?
To what end is the coming and going
The rapidly cycling, the spontaneously
Informing, the calculating spherical spiral?

Come hither muses and reveal the play
To us your captive indentured playthings.
Give us the rhyme and reason for this being
That we may not suffer each the other to
Wallow in the ignorance that slowly
Cooks the marrow to a state of existential agony.
Let us see the clear line of the majestic as it
Juts magnificently before us.

Solar Dream

The cold tap of reality is rusted...shut.
It will take a cosmic sledgehammer to detach it.
In the Shadow of Hypnotized Mediocrites, I wait
For the opportunity to dispatch it.

Mary was inseminated with DNA
from an extraterrestrial race,
But the childish myths persist, and
Bad boys with lugubrious attitudes
Face-off on the oil pan of the World
Waiting for the chance to drain it.

Oh, Apollo, melt the face of the moon
Reveal the secrets of fusion
And end this madness.

The Mysterious Virtue In Accidents

There is a mysterious virtue in accidents,
Disasters and traumatic events,
And in the machinations of the insane,
The greedy and the corrupted.

The Tao is a running stream,
A body of living force that is never the same in any instant,
Always alive, moving from the Source to the Source.

We are here now and gone soon.
Some sooner than others.
Breathe deeply and behold the precious vehicle of incarnation.
In this instant, and the next, trillions of individual lives
Will come and go in this Universe;
One of countless Universes.

In a spirit of humility,
Let us be mindful of the course of human destiny
And how it is turned spectacularly and sharply
In its path to new and unseen directions,
Unfathomable in their meaning;
With the intent of the Divine remaining occult
And perplexingly rich with sentient suffering.

How right it is to grieve.
How right it is to move
With the flow of the Tao.

First Light After the New Moon

Silver sliver fingernail points
From star and bright planet
To new earth pregnant now
Expectation and hope aligned.

Silver sliver sends a shiver
Down the mountainside
Creatures in the dark
Awaiting our decision and action.

Which way my brothers and sisters?
Toward peace and sanity?
Onward into the abyss of destruction?
Prayers rise up from tiny lives.

Oh, womb of the mind of man,
Reach up with your innocence
And grasp the love that awaits
In the true heart of oneness.

"...Our own present culture has harnessed these forces in ways
that have yielded extraordinary wealth and comfort and personal
freedom. The freedom to be lords of our own tiny skull-sized kingdoms,
alone at the center of all creation."

David Foster Wallace

"Universal brotherhood rests upon the common soul.
It is because there is one soul common to all [humans],
that brotherhood, or even a common understanding is possible."

H. P. Blavatsky

Re-Cycling

The ugly beast rose up,
A mighty winter's storm
Full of pent-up and dark horror,
Grinning, chewing and spewing.
Rose up as if it were full of power.

But it was the beast's last grasp
At control of its spent ideology,
In the autumn manifestation of strife,
Heading fast to the solstice of shadow,
Destined to fertilize a new vision-version of life.

In the isolated perspective of only now,
The summer of the beast appears as a great haboob
Blowing its dusty, foul breath
Into the tiniest crevices of our lives
Grinding all to the painful crumbling death.

But soon also, the black ice of winter's beast
Is melted, revealing the green shoots of spring.
And having faced the beast head-on in the plight,
We will again grow more awake,
Remembering that dark is the mother of light.

Funnel Effect

In life like it happens with real estate,
as the amount of livable land
steadily diminishes in mass,
the price and value
rises gradually
'til it reaches
the funnel
apex
and
its

.

VI

Notes From The Soul

This Bird of Light

In the wings of Time
My soul does fly
Across the reflection of Space
Deep into the Illusion

In the folds of Love
My soul does glide
Seeking the projection of Wisdom
Upon the face of the Universe

And in Time
And in Love
In Space and in Wisdom
Flow the currents of Spirit
Ever leading
This Bird of Light
Onward, beyond
All Time
All Space
All Love
All Wisdom
Resting only in the nest
Of the Great Pure Silence
Of the One Reality.

Act of Love

Kri,
To do,
To act.
One single movement
Commands total Awareness.
Within that One
Is the essence of all Being,
And all Existence.
From the perfection
Of The Elemental Act of Cosmos
Sprang the Entire Perfect Universe.
To command perfection
In all acts
Comes from the expression of perfection
In one single movement
And seed of time,
And it's subsequent
Expansion of that one beautiful act
(For all perfection is beauty)
Into all the movements of one's being.
Let us begin therefore,
With one totally conscious and perfect act for someone else.

Bag of Crystals

As the dawn comes,
Parts of life that have been
In the darkest places,
Are revealed.

When ugliness seems
To abound
Before our eyes,
That is when we know
The light is awakening.

In the fullness of the day,
All will be seen,
And blessing occurs
when the shadows
Are vaporized,
Cleansed by the purity
Of true substance.

The Redemption of Sisyphus

Part One – The Invitation

Slogging, completely naked,
Muscled, caked in sweat and mud and clay
He came into the journey of my dream
Eternally pushing his stone up the mountainside
Remorseless, undaunted, unabashed, evincing
The same unapologetic resignation
He displayed to Zeus and to Hades
As they consigned him to time without end.

Why do you interrupt my labours, he asked?
I am here to redeem you, I replied.
One human to another.
From one who aspires to your courage
I offer my own, fresh from its unrelenting search of dying Olympus.
Relinquish your suffering
For your Gods are all dead
And now you labour in ignorance.
Now, well honored is
Your brazen disregard for the rules of heaven.
Never forgotten is your
Theft of the secrets of the almighty Ones,
Your devotion to the thirsty People of Corinth
Or how you chained death at the gates of Hell;
Cheated Thantos with your stolen life,
And emptied the underworld in the glow of its beauty.

Rest now, oh, great man
For your laurels are deep and soft.
I offer you a better life
In the heart of all things
For you alone are worthy
Of its guardianship.

There travel before the gate in a magic forest of light
And at the gate, that splendid gate;
Wrought of gold, hinged with emeralds,
With sets of diamonds, wings of rubies
And latched with a great sapphire,
Will you reside and bask
In the glow of its beauty.

Come there now and receive a new body,
Lithe and fair, winged and full of light for
There enter in all the great and small parts of the world of love.
To pay homage and receive the rest, the reverence
The nurturance, the wholing, the healing and
Blessing of the Great Mother of all beings.

There you will have your rest, slumber in peace,
Be loved and love without measure.
Follow the crystal spring
Which pours forth from the amethyst grotto
Of this underworld, clear and bubbling joyfully
Through the cave of your forgetfulness
To the light of who you are.
Come now and roll the stone away.

"Now I understand what you tried to say to me,
How you suffered for your sanity,
How you tried to set them free.
They would not listen, they did not know how.
Perhaps they'll listen now. "

Don McLean

De State of the World

Degradation inexorable.
Difficult inevitable ending.
Disaster looming.
Doom-laden.
Doubled consumption.
Decline irreversible
Dead green and blue.
Done millennium.
Delicately-unbalanced
Dryland damaged.
Dirty waters.
Dismal bleakness.
Decisive action taken for granted.
Damaged future.
De-engineered natural resources.
Diminishing ecosystems
Dynamic complex of indecisive participants
Demanding vitality.
Delayed response.

Damning patrician silence.
Denial of the facts.
Deluded governmental instrumentality.
Demeritorious conduct.
Disconnected policies.
Diversity extinct.
Documented failure.
Distribution skewed.
Devastating impact.
Developing countries suffering.
Done down deals.
Diseases emerging.
Densities increasing
Dominating dysfunctional alien floral and faunal species
Despair not.
Decease engorging.
Do more now.
Deliver the Real Goods.

And Be Free

Like flesh torn from carrion
It sears deep and bloody
Severing the heart from the head

Fragile we are it seems
Like so much mica crushed
Beneath the foot of life

The cancer is in the mind
Divorced from the knowing,
Spotless in the bastardization of time.

Careless reverie strikes
The set of mundane days
Then we are cast into the maelstrom.

Ripples of seismic clutter
Haphazardly shake the foundations
Of our unsuspecting.

Relentless in its pounding
Merciless in its timing
Rotten, creeping, foul and necrotic.

Ceaseless seeking leads this all
To the oblivion of endless egoity
And we are born to it again and again.

Touch the preexistence of now
Feel the Peace of already always
Evermore without condition

And Be Free

The Rebirthday Room

In every moment we die and are reborn into the void from
A nothingness that is the fecund, all pervading
Indivisible, preexisting, always perfected emptiness,
That is undeniably complete and total love-bliss consciousness.

Only in the room of the Divine Heart
Of this constantly appearing,
Revealed true nature of eternal, infinite, immutable happiness,
Can we find a refuge authentic enough to shed the hard
Skin of the ego's I, and make the translation to the truly real.

Let us embrace the icy fingers of the valley of separate death
That we may be reanimated beyond the shadow of seeking,
Fear and longing
Into the bright heart of devotion, compassion and endless
Forever now in recognition of our One and True Reality.

May we always know the Beloved on sight fully in every
Human, hill, animal, plant and stone, forsaking all illusions.
And may the peace that passes beyond our understanding
Be the walking path of our Sadhana
Reaching ever to the Star of Isness.
Peace.

The Pearl

The Pearl
Is in the Bowl.
I Am Here.
There is Nothing.
Reality is This.
There is no Reality.
My Presence is One.
There is no Presence.
All is One.
Nothing Is.
I Am That.
That is Not.
Is Is Not.
I does not exist,
Writes it Life upon the Sky.
The Pearl is in the Bowl!

Careless Moments

The Earth is fertile.
As many species as are here
Have come and gone
Before we were even made.

After all of us are gone
A forest will stand
In spite of our blundering
In exception to our existence.

We have our highest visions in the woods
Where only the animals can hide
In spite of our arrogance
In exception to our pride.

All is forgiven there for men and women
For nature does not hold on to anything
It silently and gently lets everything
Grow, fail and go.

There is a danger in keeping
Our thoughts to ourselves
For only in our connectedness
Can we persist beyond
The limitations of these forms.

The strength that we need
Can come from a forest
And much wisdom can be received
In touching a tree.

Trees will always live longer than we do
And in their own natural way
They've had more time to mull things over.
But telling a tree what we believe
Won't change the situations
We have created in our shortcomings
In spite of our yearnings
In exception to our pleas.

The seedy depths of our darkest secrets
Are no match for the detachment and surrender
That a green, thick and dense forest just freely gives away,
In spite of our guilt
In exception to our will.

The Moon and Stars Came to Drink at My Pond

Listen!
The moon and stars came to drink at my pond
And the palm trees whispered in the light
Coyote called to the moon to dance
Dipped his tail and the fish kissed the stars
The crickets wept with joy.

Joy!
Palm pods rustled in the dark warm wind
A barn owl kept watch in the silent night
The mice washed the sky with crystal tears
And the foxes slept warm in their burrow
Safe in dreams of wildflowers singing.

Peace!
Peace cried the old bear
For winter is fast upon us
A howling frost will soon make way
Rest now in folds of space where soul beams
Carry the limbs of the vagabond leaves .

Cry!
Somewhere far off a soft rolling river
Rocked the cranes to the salty sea
And clouds clearly sang the memoirs
Of blue whales to the rain
Come, come take my heart... too.

Despair!
A billion years she birthed all this
And we, we marred it all in a twinkling.
Should 7 generations come and pass
They will speak only with sorrow
For all that is lost, my beauties, for all that we lost.

Sunset in the Garden of the Light

Softly sinuous like the arms of a dancing woman
The evening clouds stretched across a saffron golden sky
Pointing to the secret gates of your sacred garden
Where an arbor of roses lifted their opened hearts
In praise of your loving grace
And in anticipation of your blessed presence.

There I took refuge, but alas all that remained
Was the fragrance of your sweet perfume,
Wafting into my senses until I succumbed
To the bliss of knowing only this.
That even a mere shadow of you
Is enough to intoxicate even the least of your creations.

As Above So Below

Let he who has the eyes that see come forward and reveal the way.
Fear not the vision of truth though the way be fraught with peril.
Though you be blind, the ONE reality touches all the same.
Being that, move only in the silent knowing that the ALL is all.

Sleep no more and carry on the work of the soul that abides.
Discover reality and be free of past, present and future.
Peace floats in the voice that utters eternity, and it is you.
Die daily to all concepts and dogma to receive the true you.

Samadhi is present in the eyes of a frog
And the chattering of cicadas.
The ONE who knows moves across the face of the deep
In perfect geometry.
Release the attachment to the mind matrix
And be the fluid nature.
Oh, great truth, allow us the eyes that see
And the ears that hear.

You yourself in the entirety are the source of the ONE reality.
Religion is both a chalice of truth
And the liability of an anathema.
The golden ratio describes both the content
And form of this reality.
Evolution abides, yes, singularly exists
In the spirillae of the crystalline nature.

Correspondence describes the pattern of reality at every level.
Pass though the gateless gate of truth and be at peace.

VII

No More War

The Patriots

I
[The Beginning]

Drawn down in Lexington and Concord
Sunrise sons of liberty
Sunrise sons of liberty
Set to stage the fight to free
Not knowing how they'd conquer.

How many fell at Bunker Hill
Four hundred there they say
Four hundred there they say
Shed their blood that day
Stood their ground, resolved their will.

Full measure of their lives they gave
Only in their defense
Only in their defense
Forbid that they should hence
Transgress in an aggressor wave

Centuries now on sacred ground we stand
All now in heart we still factor
All now in heart we still factor
We'll not abide a detractor
That what they did will full expand
That what they did will full expand

II
[The Present]

Born to it and devoted,
Thought graceful and proud,
Thought graceful and proud,
You pace, sullen and loud,
Voice cracking, tongue thick and coated.

You tell of unspeakable
Horrors we will never know,
Horrors we will never know,
Phosphenes dance and glow
Emitted by scorched optic nerves unreachable.

On the battlefield of oblivion
The greatest measure you gave,
The greatest measure you gave,
Lost limb and sight, you rave,
Life sucked from the marrow, never young again.

Great spirit was required
And given freely in daylight
And given freely in daylight
Now you hide in dark, in fright

Phantoms call out the pain
Conversing with your ghost
Conversing with your ghost
Extracting the remnant host
Excruciating all that remains, a shriveling stain.

We give thanks in dollars and cents
As we race in disregard
As we race in disregard
For the lives that we discard
Broken worlds, lost love and lives of innocents.

Ahimsa

War is everywhere.
It's in the world continuously without cessation,
Deeply embedded in our history as a race,
In the news,
In the way we relate to each other,
In our words,
In the way we think about the world, the news and each other.
It's stored in the memory of our cells,
In the genetic code transmitted by our ancestors,
In the way we manufacture, sell and buy.
In the way we use and discard,
In the way we make decisions about our families and ourselves,
It's in our community in the way
That politics are acted on and lived out,
There is always a difference that is interpreted
As better or worse among us.
Is it any surprise that it is so difficult to eradicate?
When our thought and our words and our actions
Become nonviolent,
When a quantum of us is completely harmless
To the core of our beings
Only then will war disappear,
For it will have no place to find a footing,
A grasp in our minds.
A place for words as weapons to arise,
Or movement in the body to actualize.

One can practice this.
But success is only achieved
By knowing without the mind.
Here is the way:
It is the sound of the sun shining.

Southeast Asia Trilogy

#1
TELEGRAM TO MRS. SARGENT

ONLY MUDDY BOOTS AND HELMETS CAKED
RUSTING ROTTING IN STEAMING GREENHOUSES
STICK UP FROM DECAYED REMAINS CAUSED BY
DETESTABLE HUMAN ANGER VENT BY WORLD
POLITICAL COMPANY FOUNDED ON INORDINATE
DESIRE. STOP. BLUE POWDER SMOKE SIFTS
THROUGH THIN LIGHT RAYS AMONG MANY
OTHERS YOUR SON ARRIVED HERE TODAY
SHORTLY AFTER MORTAR FIRE STOPPED ON
PHNOM PENH. STOP.
                GOD

Southeast Asia Trilogy

2

VICTIM'S NIGHTMARE

He awoke screaming; clutching the stump;
Shivering in cold
Sweat. His young wife did not stir;
He was used to that by now.
Crutches carried him to the naked lightbulb kitchen.

The dream was always the same:
Three weeks walking point on a jungle patrol
Ending with a hamburger mine
And a helicopter ride.
He wondered how long the 3500 doses of
V.A. aspirin would last, chased a couple down with O.J., and
Poled himself back to bed.

He thought of the job interview he had in the morning; job
Interview number 29. His wife lay there...still;
Tears rolled across closed eyelids onto the yellowed pillowcase.

Southeast Asia Trilogy

#3

I stayed behind, you had to go
Into that distant land.
What happened to you there my friend
I could not understand.

A frightening storm
Blew you off the course
That once was
Bright and clear.

The lightning singed deep
Creases in your brow,
And thunder
Cracked your ears.

Now like some peg-legged pirate
I see you raging
In the night, as terror visions
Bind your life.

Drugged and drunken,
Lost in flight,
With demons I will never know,
And horrors I can't fight.

SMOKING (aka Body Bag Detail)

I never did it before.
I couldn't stop afterwards.
It was the smell.
Well, maybe it was more than the smell.
I shook all night
After they told me about the duty.
In the morning I stood
At attention in the detail
As the sergeant explained the routine.
I could feel the tremor.
It was like the after effects of bad weed.
They were heavier than I imagined.
It gave a real new meaning
To the saying, "dead weight."
Some leaked pink, red, yellow, green, brown, black.
Pink, red, yellow, green, brown, black.
That day I puked six times,
Thought I would pass out three times.
But I didn't.
I smoked.
It helped.
After that, I was never without one in my mouth
Unless there were officers around.

And they just kept on rolling in,
One truck after another,
And we loaded them onto a roller conveyor
Into the plane;
Each one draped with the flag.
We had boxes of those.
I counted at first.
I tried to see their faces in my mind
And to see the car
Driving up to their families' houses
The grief in their eyes.
I wanted to know why;
This wasn't right I thought.
It gave me nightmares.
So then I stopped thinking about it.
But I kept on smoking.
Still do it.
Got a cough.
Can't stop.
Sometimes I think the smell might come back,
Or the other stuff.
Oh, I don't go to funerals

On Reading An Essay About Christian Militant Fundamentalism

Just when you thought you had a clue.
It's much worse than you ever knew.
If there's a resolution here,
It's not to give the way to fear.

The refuge of my heart is all
That bides intact to heed the call
Of love's sweet rendering of worldly chill:
I can, I do, I care, I will.

The pledge of every bodhisattva
Goes beyond a lotus mantra
It stills the mind to such degree
That bliss is all that's left to be.

And so I wish the calm of peace
To every wave of fond caprice
That leads you yon away from couth
May all your life be led by Truth.

Neverland

In the dark by the pass of evening
Slinking through the inky space
Between the hypnogogic passage
To unconsciousness
And the dawn of the awakening
Grief was stolen
And replaced summarily with
Unrequited rage.
Dumbfounded in disbelief
Confounded in consternation
Rocketed into the void
Of the unthinkable
Targeted by a force
So alien to humankind
That it masquerades as peace
And stealthily commandeers the heart
To the work of war

Come one, come all
Face the fire of now
Search for the seed of truth
And find it lacking
Go to the source of rain
Falling blisteringly hard
On the backs of those
Who have chosen to protect Us
Return now my fallen angels

Retreat to the graves your mothers
Have lain with the garlands of your youth
Now our tears will fall and fall and fall
Long time will we mourn
But the emptiness will not be filled
Justice will woo only
If we come from this with
These words of wisdom upon our lips:

Never, never, never again.

Messages to the President

Part One
[On Imminent Choices], February 3, 2003

Before the Peace of Understanding comes,
Lightly on the coattails of grief;
After the raging of inordinate greed for power leaves,
Smashed upon the children of this world
Many bodies will be piled up in your name.
This will be your legacy.

Here in the House of Pain we pace and we scream,
"Is there no relief from this madness?"
"Can we not come to a pass of forbearance
Before the Logos tolerates us no longer?"
What is the meaning of love if not to sacrifice
Ones own heart to the pyre of forgiveness?
This is your opportunity to touch your soul and remember.

I bleed, I sweat blood, I come with my entrails unfolded
On the lawn of your consciousness,
Begging for a morsel of tolerance.
I am not proud, I cannot stand tall in the face of the world
As you hurry the silent ranks into the position of attack.
There is no honor in the manufacture of historical context.
Allow the people you are about to kill to enter
The core of your being
Feel their humanity, their hopes, fears, and love.
Then think again.

Never again will you pass this way and neither will we.
Let us leave a gift of wisdom so profound
That it will rock the Universe into a new order.

Part Two

[On living and dying by the sword]
September 11, 2004

Accosted by the senseless and horrific reality
You forced on the vital energy of the world
And its peoples,
I kneel numbed before the powers of the Universe,
To query the meaning of your continued existence.
For now many bodies are
Piled up in your name.
Your legacy is sealed and rests
With such great names as should not be named [Adolph Hitler,
Mao Tse Tung, Pol Pot, Idi Amin, Joseph Stalin, and yes, Saddam
Hussein]
In your thought, words and deeds,
You did and have continued to candle into life,
Creations of Horror and Terror,
None the less than these.
In choosing the path of violence and death
You mark yourself as one of them,
And have secured for yourself,
The Mark of Cain.
Here in the House of Pain
We are struck dumb.

Still the Logos tolerates you
As one of the children of Earth
So now I pray that the spirits
Of all of the children killed
Because of your life
Speak and sing and chant
Their hearts grief
Into the core of your soul
Until it bursts in shame!
And that your dreams be full of the private movies
Of woe and suffering
That your ministrations of power
Have wrought
Until you see a way clear
To love.

Scorn of Alaric

I will not die on your battlefield.

I will not cry for your brides.

A horde of wolves will come out on that grey day,

    And recruit the raptors to carry off

    The heap of your loose bellies.

Neither wise nor mad man could convince me that your hypocrisy was worthy.

So take your plastic flowers and your plastic Jesus and rage against the night.

The GOD of Abraham laughs!

Alaric holds you in contempt;

Even from 200 feet below the ground, and 2 thousand years past.

Political Science

Spin and kill and fall
Spin and kill and fall
All the grim soldiers
All the nameless men
All the silent ladies
All the sad children

Spin and kill and fall
Spin and kill and fall
Nothing can stop them all
From dying in the yard
Swinging their souls upward
No one has stopped the killing
None so far have been willing
To stop the life that's spilling
Spin and kill and fall
Spin and kill and fall

Spin and kill and fall
Spin and kill and fall
All the grim soldiers
All the nameless men
All the silent ladies
All the sad children
Spin and kill and fall

Spin and kill and fall
Be they short or be they tall
Constant pain is in the frame
Lame and still, a cause for shame
No one sees you bleed them
No one comes to free them
The light in there is so dim
Spin and kill and fall
Spin and kill and fall

Spin and kill and fall
Spin and kill and fall
All the grim soldiers
All the nameless men
All the silent ladies
All the sad children

Spin and kill and fall
Spin and kill and fall
Invest in oil
Buy the soil
Lead others to toil
Be the snake in their path
No wizardry to do the math
Just reap the after wrath
Spin and kill and fall
Spin and kill and fall
Spin and kill and fall
Spin and kill and fall
All the grim soldiers
All the nameless men

All the silent ladies
All the sad children

Put it in perspective
How much notice
Will the cosmos take?
As close as
Standing on the moon with
The best telescope
Attempting to view us
As we do our worst
You would probably see
Nothing – so
Spin and kill and fall
Spin and kill and fall

The War in Iraq – Tree of Death

Atrocity
Atrocity, Atrocity
Atrocity, Atrocity, Atrocity
Atrocity, Atrocity, Atrocity, Atrocity
Atrocity, Atrocity, Atrocity, Atrocity, Atrocity
Atrocity, Atrocity, Atrocity, Atrocity, Atrocity, Atrocity
Atrocity, Atrocity, Atrocity, Atrocity, Atrocity, Atrocity Atrocity
Atrocity, Atrocity, Atrocity, Atrocity, Atrocity, Atrocity Atrocity, Atrocity
Atrocity, Atrocity, Atrocity, Atrocity, Atrocity, Atrocity Atrocity
Atrocity, Atrocity, Atrocity, Atrocity, Atrocity, Atrocity
Atrocity, Atrocity, Atrocity, Atrocity, Atrocity
Atrocity, Atrocity, Atrocity, Atrocity
Atrocity, Atrocity, Atrocity
Atrocity, Atrocity
Atrocity
Atrocity, Atrocity
Atrocity, Atrocity, Atrocity
Atrocity, Atrocity, Atrocity, Atrocity
Atrocity, Atrocity, Atrocity, Atrocity, Atrocity
Atrocity, Atrocity, Atrocity, Atrocity, Atrocity, Atrocity
Atrocity, Atrocity, Atrocity, Atrocity, Atrocity, Atrocity Atrocity
Atrocity, Atrocity, Atrocity, Atrocity, Atrocity, Atrocity Atrocity, Atrocity
Atrocity, Atrocity, Atrocity, Atrocity, Atrocity, Atrocity Atrocity, Atrocity,
Atrocity, Atrocity, Atrocity, Atrocity, Atrocity, Atrocity Atrocity
Atrocity, Atrocity, Atrocity, Atrocity, Atrocity, Atrocity
Atrocity, Atrocity, Atrocity, Atrocity, Atrocity
Atrocity, Atrocity, Atrocity, Atrocity
Atrocity, Atrocity, Atrocity
Atrocity, Atrocity
Atrocity
Atrocity, Atrocity
Atrocity, Atrocity
Atrocity, Atrocity
Atrocity, Atrocity
Atrocity, Atrocity
Atrocity, Atrocity
Atrocity, Atrocity
Atrocity, Atrocity

VIII

The Lovers

OVER

Solace rides like a broomwind
Across my disconsolate brain,
As we finally end
This contorted masquerade;
A floor much in need of sweeping.
Our bruised opinions will mend,
Heart's blindness offset,
And I will admit to artlessness
And a weakness for your flesh.

A Christmas Morning Prayer

For only one desire:
To have Christ borning
While we have slept
With lovers' fire
Deep within the heart of us,
And mark this morning
Awakening with His Love in our eyes
For this aching world,
Our weary souls,
And the unborn yet to come;
This is my prayer.

Epilogue

Lover, burden not yourself
With sadness nor with sorrow,
For this road never ends,
It goes on forever.

And with each day, each new day,
New love and power stream forth
From your head, heart and loins.

Many things you have been
To many people; wife, mother,
Friend and lover.
From all of these, many things
You have gathered.

So, as you continue this long journey,
Take with you
Only that to give,
Which has given you joy!
The love from your lives!
The wisdom from your children!
And the youth from your eternally
New and beautiful mind.
Give of these to all who seek
Truth, Love and Peace,
And even with no thought to self,
You shall always walk in sunlight
Heart-full and strong.

Rhythm of Your Love

I cast my net into the ocean,
But only muddy sand and broken shells returned.
In the depths of it, it mocks me, the cockles and the urchin's laughter,
Piteous in their concert of faces without tears.
I cried for you, but you were not there to see it.
And I was not there to feel the waves of your pain.
Skyward I threw my head back. Silent screams
Traced the memory of your softness through the sea foam,
The curve of your velvet thigh entwining my dream.
Your breasts caressed my face, buoys in the darkness
And your delight crashed in my ears like a thousand stars
Shining in the deep, and then nothing but sighs.

Starlit seas take me home.
Rhythm of your love pounds me.
Starlit seas wake me soon.
Rhythm of your love finds me.

I didn't even remember your name, but I loved you.
In the ebb and eddies of your smiles and the motherly
Way you stood welcoming, receiving my grief
Your sapphire eyes burned into my heart
Like molten lava surging through the ocean floor
Steaming the water so deep,

That it cooled before it rose to the surface.
Your tears salted my skin and I can still taste it.
The fish slip quickly glittering the horizon of my love
And littering the silver shadows with false diamonds
Cascade after cascade of thought penetrates to the ethers
Of your footprints, and the void drinks me until I am
Empty and lost in Oblivion.

Starlit seas take me home.
Rhythm of your love pounds me.
Starlit seas wake me soon.
Rhythm of your love finds me.

Starlit seas take me home.
Rhythm of your love pounds me.
Starlit seas wake me soon.
Rhythm of your love finds me.

Christmas Full Moon Poem 12/24/1996

In my heart of hearts, I love you so.
So clearly now I'd have you know of my devotion.

So cast with me your fear away.
Come dance with me, come out and play – Spirit in motion.

Shadows in the firelight flicker.
We laugh and cry and then we snicker with tender notion.

The moon is rising. Lights your face.
Full blossoms love, reveals your grace, your gentle potion.

Auspiciously we came to steer
Our vessel fair to waters clear; a Dolphin's ocean.

Now lets us with reason weigh
The gift of being here this day, Life's soothing lotion.

For time is now, there is no other
Loves simple task entrains the mother of the universal unction.

IX

The Haiku

1980 Haiku

Chinese lanterns dance
Arrhythmic lines, propelled by
Warm sweet harbinger.

Anteater's dinner
Searching food on brown and green:
Lilac branch and leaf.

The sluggish fly falls.
Night leaves sift. Withered phlox shrinks:
Standing brown soldiers.

Small bundle of boy
Rolls like a ball down log hill;
Covered with white rain.

Seasonal

Night windmass surging
Stirring out pungent spirits
Banishing green grail

Satin white skin shines
Rose hearts beating out rhythm
Music chilly night

Industrious wench
Miller moth moon tolerates
Flower explosion

Contempt for rock silence
Bursting soil and transforming
Seed articulation

Swan Repose

Great swan spreads its wings
The face of the omniverse
Manifesting all.

Perception binds life
To identification,
Forever seamless.

In the tree of life
And knowledge lies bliss measured
Only by starlight.

Can one know both ways?
Or is it a mirrored view
Cast loosely in twain?

In the depth of soul
The One only can know it,
And mystery rules.

2005

Healing hands rest
Here bind chaos, flow it out
Leave stillness and grace.

Electrical phase
Switch on, integrate light waves
Bounce up to the soul

Weary traveler
Eases down amber silence
Into settled ahhh!

Tears of joy come now
Gratitude for release of
Superfluity.

Fall Haiku 2009

The rollicking wind
Spread the gold leaves in earnest
Blanketing my heart.

Sharad Purnima Haiku

Eat the moon pie whole
Bursting in delicious mouths
Pastry of the Gods!

PLACE AND TIME INDEX

Title

The Poet
Poetry Lesson #2
Epitaph
Gordian Maze
Lynx Rufus
Organ Riddle
Wasusu Landscape
Schrodinger's Dream: Natures Answer
What Quadravitatis Sees
Cheetah
Butterfly
Did You See the Morning?
Little Bear, Laughing Raven
The Copperheads
The Doldrums
Snake Eyes
July 4
We Sat In The Park
A Walk In the Snow
Forever Magic
Friendvessel
Invocation
In The House Of My Belonging
In This Circle I Belong
About A Life…A Work In Progress
A Transition
Weatherman
Geisha
Eldila
Chief Joseph

Place	Date
Triangle Park, Boulder Colorado	Summer 1969
Cottonwood, Arizona	June 21, 2002
Cottonwood, Arizona	May 6, 2008
Colorado Springs, Colorado	1979
Tucson, Arizona	November 22, 2002
Colorado Springs, Colorado	1979
Colorado Springs, Colorado	1980
Colorado Springs, Colorado	1979
Squaw Pass, Colorado	1989
Buffalo Creek, Colorado	1990
Cottonwood, Arizona	May 5, 1997
Cottonwood, Arizona	July 7, 2007
Cottonwood, Arizona	April 20, 2008
Cottonwood, Arizona	December 11, 2004
Cottonwood, Arizona	May 4, 2007
Cottonwood, Arizona	October 1, 2004
Sedona, Arizona	July 4, 2017
Boulder, Colorado	Summer 1970
Colorado Springs, Colorado	February 2, 1978
Colorado Springs, Colorado	Summer 1979
Denver, Colorado	1987
Denver, Colorado	August 27, 1991
Sedona, Arizona	1998
Cottonwood, Arizona	March 19, 2003
Cottonwood, Arizona	2004
Denver, Colorado	1990
Colorado Springs, Colorado	1978
Colorado Springs, Colorado	1979
Colorado Springs, Colorado	1976
Colorado Springs, Colorado	1979

Title

A Master
The Hospice Candidate
Holy Man: He Who Knows Love
Speak Of It Then
Venus in Tights
Rocking With The Wind
New Horizons
Connected
The Sacredness Of Porpoises
In The Darkness Of The New Moon
Solar Dream
The Mysterious Virtue In Accidents
First Light After The New Moon
Re-Cycling
Funnel Effect
This Bird of Light
Act of Love
Bag of Crystals
The Redemption of Sisyphus
De State Of The World
And Be Free
The Rebirthday Room
The Pearl
Careless Moments
The Moon and Stars
    Came to Drink at My Pond
Sunset in the Garden of the Light
As Above So Below
Ahimsa
The Patriots
Southeast Asia Trilogy #1
Southeast Asia Trilogy #2
Southeast Asia Trilogy #3

Place	Date
Colorado Springs, Colorado	1977
Sedona, Arizona	2003
Cottonwood, Arizona	Valentine's Day 2008
Tulsa, Oklahoma	April 1992
Cottonwood, Arizona	October 31, 2007
Cottonwood, Arizona	1999
Cottonwood, Arizona	July, 22, 2000
Cottonwood, Arizona	March 7, 2000
Cottonwood, Arizona	September 20, 2004
Cottonwood, Arizona	May 29, 2005
Cottonwood, Arizona	November 2002
Cottonwood, Arizona	January 12, 2005
Cottonwood, Arizona	January 28, 2009
Sedona, Arizona	January 4, 2018
Cottonwood, Arizona	2009
Cottonwood, Arizona	2003
Cottonwood, Arizona	1995
Cottonwood, Arizona	May 17th, 2003
Oak Creek Canyon, Arizona	June, 2003
Cottonwood, Arizona	2005
Cottonwood, Arizona	2005
Cottonwood, Arizona	October 10, 2005
Cottonwood, Arizona	March 5, 2006
Cottonwood, Arizona	October, 13, 2006
Cottonwood, Arizona	2003
Cottonwood, Arizona	May 1, 2009
Cottonwood, Arizona	January 19, 2019
Sedona, Arizona	2004
Sedona, Arizona	July 4, 2008
Colorado Springs, Colorado	1976
Colorado Springs, Colorado	1976
Flight from Phoenix to Puerto Vallarta	October 18, 1992

Title

Place	Date
Cottonwood, Arizona	October 2003
Cottonwood, Arizona	2004
Cottonwood, Arizona	February 3, 2003
Cottonwood, Arizona	December 20, 2005
Denver, Colorado	1985
Cottonwood, Arizona	2003
Cottonwood, Arizona	October 7, 2006
Colorado Springs, Colorado	1979
Denver, Colorado	December 25, 1989
Cottonwood, Arizona	2003
Cottonwood, Arizona	2003
Cottonwood, Arizona	December 24, 1996
Colorado Springs, Colorado	1980
Cottonwood, Arizona	Spring 1991-Summer 2002
Cottonwood, Arizona	September 27, 2004
Cottonwood, Arizona	July 19, 2005
Cottonwood, Arizona	November 11, 2009
Cottonwood, Arizona	October 18, 2005
Crescent City, California	1947